SNAPCHAT MARKETING

TECHNIQUES

A Marketing BluePrint to Monetize your Followers on

SnapChat

Author: George Pain

DISCLAIMER

Copyright © 2017

All Rights Reserved

ABOUT THE AUTHOR

George Pain is an entrepreneur, author and business consultant. He specializes in setting up online businesses from scratch, investment income strategies and global mobility solutions. He has built several businesses from the ground up, and is excited to share his knowledge with readers.

TABLE OF CONTENTS

INTRODUCTION

What is Snap Chat?

Snapchat was developed in September 2011. The application has a massive user base and supports 20 languages. The interesting part is that this application is that it originated from inside of a classroom as one of the creators, Evan Spiegel, talked with his classmates about his idea for the application in April of 2011.

Why has Snap Chat Grown in Popularity?

Snapchat has grown in popularity because of its user-friendly interface. Snapchat is the brainchild of what happened with Facebook and Instagram when people were taking pictures of their meals. The problem is that Snapchat was a solution to a different portion of the problem. They offered more than taking pictures and making them look nice. Many people wanted to take the pictures and interact with them by adding filters very quickly. People didn't want to go into software like Photoshop and edit their photos to get unique items on their picture. In fact, most of the older individuals disliked Snapchat because you get to put a whole bunch of useless stuff on an otherwise okay picture. Snapchat allowed others to play around with images that they took of themselves and to be playful in general since Snapchat is geared towards the younger generation. This naturally meant that they picked it up with ease and we know the story of Snapchat from there.

Why Snap Chat is a Great Way to get Easy Adverts

Snapchat is great when it comes to advertising because of its low barrier to entry compared to other social media platforms. A Facebook advertisement meant that you might need to test different advertisements to create a much larger advertising campaign that will be more successful in the end game. With Snapchat, you don't really have to do all that complicated research because you just have to look around for groups that fit the product that you're trying to sell. In other words, it's the difference between looking at an academic book and reading a fictional novel. Snapchat is a fantastic way to deploy advertisements because they are short, they reach a very wide audience of individuals, and Snapchat is currently the new hottest social media page with which you can easily just take a picture of your product, add some filters, and send it out to get massive success in selling that product if you hit the correct market for it.

Success Rates with Snapchat Adverts

The success rate of an advertisement on Snapchat is remarkable with marketers getting up to 50% click rate for an advertisement if their brand is a known product. If your product isn't really known on the market, but you have a very interesting and interactive advertisement that individuals will flock to, you can see rates of 30% to 40% which is massive when it comes to advertising campaigns. Snapchat also allows you to advertise in more unique ways that you might not have had access to whenever you utilized Facebook and YouTube. For instance, you can gather your own followers in a Snapchat profile that fits the niche that you're trying to sell towards and simply send out a post that is shared amongst those users. Then the same post is shared from those users to other users who might like the same contact. This is essentially a free form of advertising that only costs your time. However, we will go ahead and cover these options later in this book.

ATTRACTING FOLLOWERS USING SNAPCHAT

Finding Your Niche

You won't get anywhere if you don't find the correct niche for what

you're trying to advertise to. Snapchat is a very enclosed system, but it

also allows people to discover others via the Discover tab. This means

that unless you fit the specific niche that the individual is looking for

inside of the Discover tab, you are not likely to get any followers on

your Snapchat profile. The importance of getting followers on your

Snapchat profile is that they are your advertising audience. Sure, there

are options for you to mass advertise for thousands of dollars on the

Discover page of the Snapchat application, but your core audience is

what drives the advertising on your Snapchat profile. In other words, if

you find the correct niche you will need to adapt yourself so that you

retain those followers. This also means that you need to have multiple profiles if you intend to have multiple niches. Now, that isn't to say that you can't just have one profile and advertise to everything but if you plan to do the advertising yourself (for the most part) you are going to want to have several different profiles dedicated to several different niches. We will talk about how you can utilize others to advertise in the niche that you want without having to create your own niche profile but if you're just getting started on Snapchat, you want to find the niche that is currently popular for you and begin from there.

Paying Other Snap Chat Users

Now there is an excellent way to compensate for the inability to advertise to everybody because your pockets aren't completely bottomless. You do have a secondary option that you can utilize that will use some money but will allow you to contact those in the niches you are trying to hit. You see, there are many people who have followers in niches that are average, and these are people that have thousands to tens of thousands of followers that don't normally get the same recognition from Brand companies as people who have hundreds of thousands to millions of people. This means that you are truly capable of advertising in an area that was previously untapped by Major organizations beforehand beyond the Discover page. Ideally, when you first start out you want to hit the profiles that only have a thousand or so views and you don't really want to negotiate with those that have tens of thousands of views. The reason is because the ones with thousands of views are less likely to have begun to get recognition by other individuals utilizing the tactics that you are learning in this book. They haven't gotten used to the advertising game and you are trying to take advantage of that at this point. When you reach those individuals who have thousands of followers, you are more likely to encounter negotiations. The ones that have thousands of individuals don't know what they're worth yet most of the time, so you are likely to save more money by going towards these individuals than you are with the upper echelons of popularity. Having said that, there is also a secondary benefit when it comes to advertising with these profiles because you begin to understand your audience much better when you try to hit a niche in a small area and see if that hit is either very popular or very low in popularity. You see, these smaller profiles are also less likely to have individuals that are susceptible to the mass targeting that one normally associates with a profile that's meant for advertising. This means that you can truly get the analytics you need when it comes to whether the crowd you are targeting is interested in your product or not. It allows you to do small time advertising to test out products to see just how popular an area of the market might be. This leads into my next point.

Converting A Mailing List

On Snapchat, mailing lists can go one of two ways or both ways depending on what you plan to do with your Snapchat account. You see, Snapchat itself can act as a mailing list simply because all mailing list is just a list of emails that you send out a message to whenever you have a product that you're selling or a newsletter that updates them on important features of products. Snapchat is almost no different except that it's a video and camera footage rather than textual based notification, so it just has to be adapted for that. When you first come into Snapchat, you are required to sign up and you are then given something called your snap code. This is a type of QR code that other

Snapchat users can download via a QR Reader. The beauty about this is that it is very easy to take this image, save it, and then share it amongst those who might have a Snapchat account and is already on the mailing list that exists right now. This means that you could intermingle the crowds that are on your mailing list as well as the crowds that are on your Snapchat account. Having said that, the difference between the two is pretty big. You see, with Snapchat you're not going to be able to make fancy email templates that you can follow every single time and we'll talk about the exact type of content that you want to have inside of each Snapchat, but the honest truth is that it's not going to be something that you can repeat or replicate every single time. It's not a monthly newsletter and it's not something that you can pre-format because almost all of Snapchat is based around organic or, rather, real material. This means that you can't replicate the same advertisement in the exact same way that you sent out the first one, but this also works to your advantage. This means that the individuals on Snapchat are willing to engage with you a lot more than the individuals on your standard mailing list. After a long time has passed, emails on the mailing list either become useless because people are no longer using them, or they have filtered out your email long ago. On Snapchat, you know when people are no longer paying attention to your snaps because they stop following you or they stop reacting to the snaps that you put up. This means that you'll get far more interaction when it comes to engaging your audience via Snapchat than you probably ever had while engaging with them over email. As I said, when you begin, you get a QR code that others can scan, and this is another form of conversion that you can utilize. You can redesign your business card with the snap code on the back of the business card so that individuals that you hand your card to can turn it over and take a picture of it in order to follow you on Snapchat. This is one of the first ways you could ever communicate with such a large crowd utilizing business cards. There are normally two items on a business card that everyone knows of and that is the phone number and the e-mail address that you use but with Snapchat, they can interact with your social media account on your Snapchat Channel. This is a first when it comes to the social media network form of advertising. Yes, you can easily get them to follow your Twitter, your Facebook, or even your LinkedIn but the honest truth is that these are not purely for advertising and are more for adding them towards your friends list. Snapchat, on the other hand, is more geared towards business.

Sharing Discount Coupons

If you already have a line of products, then you have a way to turn customers onto your Snapchat account because if you attach a discount to those products, you can then send out an email to those who are currently following you on your email list saying that they will get a discount for following you on the Snapchat. This is an excellent way to get individuals who are normally on the Snapchat platform to not only switch over to your Snapchat account but also purchase the product that you're selling. Depending on your Market, you may be in for a huge conversion rate if you attempt to do this. The reason why is because if you are an Amazon Kindle seller as well as a Snapchat Advertiser, you have a very interesting combination of audiences that take up most of these areas. Users of both platforms are normally younger girls that use Kindle and their new smartphones to share their experiences and to enjoy the experiences of others. In fact, one of the biggest markets on the Kindle is female romance because most of the individuals purchasing books for their Kindles are female. So, romance is a huge genre that specifically targets female audience members most of the time. That doesn't mean that there aren't some romances for men but it's not exactly something that you hear about every day and when you do hear about it, it usually raises an eyebrow. There is a difference between these two groups because the people who are on the Kindle range from the early twenties to about the late forties while those on the Snapchat platform are in the early teenage years to the late twenties. As you can see, this creates a huge gap in terms of age but if you have that audience that is in The Sweet Spot between twenty and their late twenties, you can actually get an explosion of converted members that were once following your email list that are also now following your Snapchat.

CREATING CONTENT FOR SNAPCHAT

Know Your Rules

The first thing that you must know about creating content for Snapchat is that you have a new set of rules and it's a little bit different to the other applications that you may have advertised on before. You see, if I had given you a guide on advertising on Snapchat a year before hand, I would be giving you a completely different guide than the one you're receiving now. Snapchat regularly updates its' user interface so that it is more slick, easier to use, and a lot friendlier than the last update, so they say. The point is that you need to understand that you need to follow Snapchat updates regularly and adapt your strategy. This is different from Facebook or YouTube where the individual was primarily able to create a static image or a video and then release it on the network by choosing which areas they wanted to advertise it. Snapchat is a little bit different because the way you organize around people and the way your advertising is carried out in Snapchat is different than Facebook or

YouTube. In Snapchat, you have a Discover tab, which is what the high-end advertising agencies would go towards if they are a big-name brand. The problem is that most small businesses simply can't afford the triple digit figure that Snapchat wants in order to just get a small window of time on this spot. Snapchat is going to show this to every single user that's on the Snapchat platform, so they want to make as much money off this single spot as possible, so it is literally almost impossible for the average small business holder to get into the spot, but we'll talk about that a little bit later. Right now, I want to talk about how the actual advertising game goes and we'll explain this in a little bit more depth later in this book. What you need to understand is that in Facebook, you would choose a category that you wanted to advertise to and an age group that you might want to advertise to. In Snapchat, you look around for groups that fit those descriptions and then you find a way to advertise towards those groups. This is what makes Snapchat so much different in comparison to platforms like Facebook and YouTube where the advertising market is a click-of-a button away rather than some researched infiltration of a group. You must know your rules in

19

order to navigate the Snapchat space and to advertise to the individuals using the Snapchat platform. This does not mean you need to know your marketing rules, it just means that you need to actually know how to use this application before you start sending adverts over it. Therefore, I highly suggest you create your own, separate account so that you can get a feel for how you navigate inside of the platform and how others will see you as the application you are.

Make Sure it is Organic

Let's go ahead and talk about the differences in the types of advertisements that you're going to be releasing on the Snapchat platform and how they are different from the ones that you may have released on Facebook or YouTube. On Snapchat, the advertisements must be organic in order for them to work and what I mean by organic is that it has to seem like a real person is behind the account rather than a big-name company. The odds of an individual clicking on an advertisement made by a big-name company is actually pretty low on the Discover page. The Discover pages are made up of these five to six "stories" on the Side Bar and a main splash page that you see and everyone else sees. If you plan to advertise in the Snapchat way, you must seem like you're a real user that is invested in the people that you're advertising to. This means that if you plan on advertising a book that you may have written, you won't advertise it in the similar fashion of simply uploading an image of the book with a review and sending it out over Facebook. Additionally, you may not appear in a YouTube video where you are talking about the themes of your books and how you believe it relates to you. I'm not saying that anyone has made that type of advertisement or that anyone hasn't, but the point is that the material that you make should be something like you taking a picture of yourself while reading the book and the book title is clearly in view or you take a selfie while someone else reads the book behind you and they're not paying attention to what you're doing. These types of advertisements are what are known as organic advertisements or advertisements that seem like they could possibly happen in real life rather than a studio. The faker it seems to the customer or the person that's going to be seeing it on the Snapchat platform, the more likely that that individual is going to ignore the advertisement.

Make Sure It Matches the Niche

Just as the advertisement has to be organic, it also has to fit the area that you're advertising to. Unlike Facebook, where you get the court advantage of being able to select the categories that your advertisements fit, Snapchat makes it so that you have to search out the audiences that fit your advertisement on their platform. If it doesn't fit the niche then the odds of them actually being interested in it are rather slim and if you spent money while trying to run an advertisement on somebody else's profile or trying to get it through a mailing list that you have on your Snapchat, you are likely to have spent all that effort for maybe one to two clicks at the most with give or take tens to hundreds depending on how big your mailing list is in the beginning. This means that you need to go on the Discover page and actually discover groups that are specifically designed around that niche and begin to follow people who have big followers and contribute to the platform regularly. We'll talk about this a little bit later on but just make sure that the advertisement is not only organic, but it also fits inside of the realm that you're advertising too.

PRE-SELLING ON SNAPCHAT

Vague Pre-launch Adverts

The thing that you need to understand about the younger audience on Snapchat is that this younger audience loves the build-up much more than the ability to instant click. If you are trying to pre-sell an item as hard as you can, then you want to first start off with an organic advertisement that is as vague as you could possibly be while also being able to introduce your product. This is because the user is going to see your organic advertisement and wonder where that advertisement came from in terms of telling a story. The truth of the matter is that you should also include a QR code at the end of every video if you can possibly do this but it's not entirely plausible for everybody that's actually doing it. Great research went into the design of Snapchat and this research was only available in the past ten or so years due to the fact that we had several privacy options during that time. Nowadays, you can barely leave the house without someone sending you a notification of some kind saying that the military

23

enlistment has ended, the pie shop is back open, and the couple that had previously ordered in the top apartment above you were not home. The reason why this research is absolutely vital whenever you're selling your advertisements is due to the fact that younger kids do indeed press on the buy button a lot quicker and seem to not stay on the web page for more than a couple of seconds. At the same time these younger kids also can analyze an advertisement when they are looking at a screen. Research has actually shown that kids are far more susceptible to press more of your buy buttons if you extend the amount of time that you are advertising for. If you decide to send out your vague advertisement the day before the pre-sale happens, then you're likely losing a lot of customers but if you set the pre-sell date a month from now, then you will have people coming in from all over in order to purchase the product that you're trying to sell towards the younger crowds. This actually brings me to my next topic.

Good Negatives

This brings me to the issues that you want to avoid on Snapchat, but they may not be what you think. You see, creating content on the

Snapchat platform can be a bad process but you may be thinking of the term bad as in the item is not worth buying but sometimes bad equals a horror movie that is on the B grade list of "Worth it to Watch it." Snapchat users love controversy but what they don't love is racism and pretty much anything that goes with feminism. So long as you stay away from racism and anything dealing with feminism really, you will have a wonderful time on Snapchat. A good example of this is a bad pun that you let air over your Snapchat profile. Most people would get rid of this before they ever sent it out but if you're the type of individual who doesn't mind being made fun of in the art of advertising unlike the other people, then accidentally making a shoot that is bad can be turned into a way to make further profits in the business that you're attempting to sell. This is what I mean by Good Negatives because there are negatives in the Snapchat world where if you produce even one of the pre-mentioned two categories, you are likely to lose most of your followers if not all of your followers. On the other hand, you also have the horrible puns and bad jokes that you could utilize to bring in individuals from the tech world, the world of artistry, and even sports.

These three categories tend to love puns and bad jokes that make the individual chuckle even though it's not absolutely hilarious. Not only does this give them a good laugh but it also allows you to make organic content that many people will bite on to because everyone loves to torture themselves with bad jokes at this age because they find the bad jokes to be somewhat hilarious even though most of us make those jokes later in life because we find that they are still funny.

Launch with Limited Quantities

There are a few tactics that you can utilize to get the Snapchat followers to click on your ads; and each of them has their own special set of circumstances where they will work and where they will not work. The first one is that you can launch with limited quantities and this is really good if you have a high-quality product that you know your audience wants. If you don't have a high-quality product that's worth hundreds of dollars that you know that your audience wants, the odds of you actually being able to sell the item is pretty low. The way you find out if the high-quality product is something that your niche wants is you literally ask them. You see, I keep saying that Snapchat is different to the forms of advertising that you might see on Facebook and on YouTube; and that is the truth because you can directly ask the individuals following you what they want from you and then you can provide them that. The problem is getting the individuals to actually sign up to your Snapchat account in the first place and for that you need a primary product. If you have a primary product and you don't have any other products, then you simply can't perform a launch with limited quantities because you need that product to bring in as many people as possible. The product that you want to utilize for launches with limited quantities is an item that is either your second product or your third product on the line. You already have the appropriate number of followers that you really want to have in order to sell that product. There are also a few different items that fit the category of being able to be sold as a limited quantity items and having a high-quality item is just one requirement in this category. These items can either be a high-tech object, such as a pair of headphones that you managed to manufacture, meant for Holiday access so that it might be something that they want to wear around during the holiday season or they want to give their loved ones because it's just that type of product, or a massive information product. The last one is the most easily accessible because all you need is just a big book or a course that you want to sell. When I'm talking about a big book I mean a book that is nearly three times the number of words that you normally provide. This is because you want them to think that whenever they buy your high-priced item at limited quantity, they are getting a better deal than if they were to purchase anything from someone else.

Offer Different Pre-Sale Rewards

Now there are two ways to handle pre-sale rewards and you see them whenever you look at video games that are provided on the mass market. You have the service of Humble Bundle, which rewards early purchasers with lower prices for the same amount of content overall. For example, if you purchase the highest tier of all of the games when the first set of games comes out then you know you will get all the games for the span of the sale. Only you spend less money than later purchasers because you probably spent close to $10 to $15 to purchase this tier but you also get rewarded for purchasing it earlier than other people by receiving additional games during the cycle of the sale. This is the first type of reward for purchasing a presale that involves offering different presale rewards. If you are selling more than one product, you can actually sell those products at a cheaper price in the beginning in order to get as many purchasers as possible. If they are the type of individual that need to wait for a paycheck, then they will be stuck with your second offer down the line that is slightly more expensive but will give them the same content. This is the best way to increase the sale price of the items that you're trying to sell without angering the consumer on the other side.

The second type of pre-sale rewards that you've seen are the ones that involve the DLCs on the consoles. These are either the upfront giant package of presale items (that can only be gathered if you bought the game beforehand) or the season's pass that will give you access to the newer maps and digital content earlier than other individuals. The most common type of implementation that you see of this with actual products that are on Kickstarter where they are granted a certain number of items depending on how much they actually donate to your cause and this brings up the next type of sale, but we'll talk about that in a moment because we're currently talking about this. Whenever you sell a high-quality product, you want to think of things that go with that product that are almost as good as that product if not better. No one wants to buy extra stuff if the extra stuff is never going to be utilized so it's just seen as a waste of money. Therefore, if you were to sell a cell phone that you developed then you want to sell high-quality headphones as a bonus to buying these cell phones earlier (something like a carrying case and protector or just generally everything that goes with a cell phone in the first place) that they would normally have to buy in the side. This brings up another aspect that you can utilize to see if you have accessories that you can sell. Cell phones normally come with a large array of additional items that are included with managing a cell phone on a daily basis and for a crowd that normally utilizes these accessories, packaging them as a reward for purchasing the pre-sale is often a very good incentive for them. Now, this is just one example of where you could sell these items but that doesn't mean that you have to be selling cell phones. The key concepts are that if you want to pre-sell items, you first need to choose whether you want to make a prolonged sale or short-term investment towards a sale. The second is whether you want to include items that are either of high-quality that meet the item in question on a personal value or provide items of convenience that would normally be an accessory to that item.

Creating Your Own Devil's Hour

A lot of businesses will have seasons where they do a special deal and it only lasts for a couple of months, but they always have those specific type of sales that happen on days that you know that something is going to happen. Everyone who has a television in the world knows what Black Friday and Cyber Monday are. This is because they are among the biggest shopping holidays that are solely focused on providing American consumers with enormous deals. So they are known to Americans as days in which they can fully gouge their wallets because they know that they're going to get a rather good deal. On the other hand, everyone except American consumers know that day is one to watch absolutely appalling insanity in the stores. You have normal people beating each other to death over televisions or people literally

31

being crushed in a crowd because they were too busy focusing on sales instead of paying attention to another human being. Americans are the butt of jokes to the international community on these days. However, the point of the matter is not how horrible Americans act during these days but the fact that these days exist and so many people know about them. They would effectively be the witching hour or the devil's hours of sales. The important part of such a day or set of days is that each of them have a special purpose and everyone knows when they happen, which means that people are capable of saving up for that event so that they can literally buy everything out. Online websites and even retail stores get into the process of preparing for these days because of how many people are willing to cause stores to become sold out over the items that the store chose to put on their Black Friday sale. You can take advantage of this and begin to set an hour in the week or a day in the month where you make an outrageous sale. A great example of a website that already does this is the website known as Udemy. This website sells educational courses on a regular basis and on Black Friday they tend to sell the most number of educational courses across-the-board where instructors earn thousands upon thousands of dollars. However, they also have a rampant problem when it comes to their courses due to the fact that they are always trying to maximize the profits that they get. Due to this, the users of this website have actually gotten used to not actually paying anything more than $20 for a course and they will usually just wait for a coupon to become available. This way, they don't have to purchase hundreds of dollars of courses.

On Snapchat, you can begin to generate sales by having a special day where you sell an item that is normally high priced at about half of the price or even 25% of the price. It could be a random item and you could also make it a limited quantities sale so that there's an even higher competition to get that item. The point is that you need to make the schedule predictable because once it is predictable, the users that are on your Snapchat following list will begin to expect that day and save up for that date to see if they want to buy whatever you are selling on that date for the crazy low price that you're selling it for. Needless to say, you do need to choose something that would normally not cost you a lot of money because otherwise you're going to lose a lot of money by trying to do this. It's best if the material is some form of digital content because then you don't have to worry about having a potential loss. However, one thing that I will say that you will notice about this is that not only will they purchase the one item that you provided in the crazy sale but 1 out of 10 times you are likely to get other purchases on the same website provided that you have prices that aren't normally crazy (like $500 for a $20 pair of headphones).

Make It Organic

The last part of the section is just a reminder that you need to make it organic and you need to keep it in line with the niche that you're selling it. After all, a knitting group is not going to Seek and Destroy cell phones whenever they're up for grabs. You need to make sure that the product that you are selling or pre-selling is going to be a product that they actually want and can use. If it is a product that they cannot use, then you are likely going to get bad reviews after you have sold it. So, it would actually do you more harm than good by selling this product and then gaining those bad reviews rather than just not selling the product at all. They must be able to utilize the item and bring that item into their everyday life. Once they bring that item into their everyday life, they can begin to recognize your brand as something that is a part of their life and once their life includes your brand, your products will begin to sell more as you begin to open and expand the lines in what you sell. This is all about creating brand recognition in the long run and so by being able to provide them with high-quality products that they can utilize in their specific niches, you not only attract the Snapchat followers that would normally come to your profile in the first place, but you also attract individuals outside of the Snapchat advertising circle simply due to the fact that the Snapchat followers will likely have provided you with Word of Mouth advertising.

SNAPCHAT PAID ADVERTISING

Paying Big Profiles Leads to More Success

Now when it comes to selling a product you might think that the default Snapchat ads are the best way to go like it is with Facebook and even YouTube. However, the truth is that Snapchat doesn't work like that. Snapchat is a personal platform where the item that you're trying to sell must be personalized. This means that if you are selling some sort of knitting kit that you think would be able to overtake some of your competition then you would likely want to look up a profile that is centered around knitting. Then contact them via their Snapchat or the email that they may give out occasionally. Now, I had already told you why you should go after the smaller groups and one of the key things to look out for in big profiles is if they have a business link for their profile because this usually means that they are already in the Snapchat advertising game and so if they think that you can be part of their exclusive circle of sponsored advertisements, then you are going to likely be paying a hefty price tag. If you are starting out and you are just wanting to use Snapchat as an easy way to advertise, I would not suggest you go after profiles that actually have an email stating that advertising companies should contact them via this email. There are profiles that request thousands of dollars to get access to the audience inside of those profiles and this is almost no different than if you were to be on the Discover page. However, there is one big benefit that comes with being advertised on a big profile that you won't get if you are on the Discover page. Those followers of that profile believe in the individual who maintains that profile and so that person who maintains the profile is a trusted member, which means that any product that they suggest is more likely to receive attention over other products because they trust that individual. It's kind of like asking your friend for advice when it comes to purchasing cars and usually trust their opinion because they've dealt with cars a lot longer than you have. You are likely going to go after the car that they suggest because you can trust their opinion and so it's very important to realize the benefit that comes with these enormous profiles.

37

Forming Advertising Circles on Niches

I already hinted at it with the previous section but once you get into Snapchat advertising you will begin to realize that there are circles of individuals who have been at this game far longer than you have and have built a small empire when it comes to advertising publicly. This actually leads you into other markets that you can advertise in and you can check out their profiles to see which markets that they are having success in. This becomes very beneficial if you are trying to look for areas to expand your own business and, most of the time, it's usually just about how you can out do the other business. The reason why you don't want to do this is because you begin to hurt the group as a whole if you begin to dig into other people's advertising areas. So you want to focus on areas that they haven't covered that you can then co-advertise when it comes to selling your products. This not only helps you in expanding your business, but it also helps the circle of advertisers that you are utilizing to help build your business. Eventually, you will grow out of needing these individuals because people will naturally just flock to your profile once they realize that these products are coming from you but for the time being, you want to work with them it to expand everybody's businesses.

Snap Ads

Snap ads are the middle man when it comes to straight advertising on the snap platform but it's actually relatively cheap in comparison to some of the other forms of advertising. For instance, many people will spend maybe $100,000 in order to reach as many people as possible on Facebook but that same advertisement on Facebook could easily just cost $3,000 on Snapchat. As you'll see in a moment, the advertisement actually makes sense across the board because even local geofilters, the cheaper of all the options, actually normally costs about the same price for the same amount of time because that price was quoted for a month. Essentially, you are allowed to send out an advertisement that gives you the ability to show a short video or just an image. It varies in price based on what option you select. These can be then transferred to the website that the advertisement is trying to get them to go to.

Snap Sponsored Lenses

Snap sponsored lenses are perhaps the most expensive part of advertising on the platform, but the honest truth is that it really works. If you are a large company that can take the deep-pocketed cost of anywhere from $450,000 to nearly a million dollars, then you can expect to get some results on the investment that you had into the platform. A good example of a company that actually spent this type of money and received an investment was Taco Bell, where over 220 million individuals actually played with the lenses. This was fantastic for Taco Bell because Taco Bell created something that had the user invested for over 20 seconds. That is a long time when it comes to advertisements considering most people are disinterested in an advertisement in the first 5 seconds as they are usually annoyed by the fact that the advertisement happened. Due to the fact that lenses are the primary way that people express themselves inside of Snapchat, using lenses to advertise products is a fantastic way to get a lot of eyes on your product.

Local Geofilters

If you are a small business and you are trying to get an audience in the city that you're in, then you have the option to utilize what are known as geofilters. These are part of the bigger class known as filters, but they let the individuals on the Snapchat application know that you are currently in an area and that you are sponsoring an event or a get together towards your Snapchat followers. The reason why I suggest this one is because it is probably the cheapest method of advertising to local environments when compared to snap ads and snap sponsored lenses. You don't need to purchase any fancy software to get access to these types of filters. This is because when you go onto the Snapchat advertising page, they will give you a link to their own creative style of filter creator that you can utilize to create your filters for whatever event that you need. The Creator will not only allow you to create your filters but then you'll just go straight into choosing the dates you want the advertisement to take place and the actual area that you want this filter to be applied to. Once you've done that, you can then submit it to the Snapchat page and it will be sent to everyone in that area and they will be able to utilize it only if they are in that area, which gives a more exclusive feel to the people who are in that area and can join that event. For instance, after having spent the time to create a custom filter for just the region that surrounds my local hospital, I was able to get a full day's geofilter for literally $140 or rather $137.26. This is very affordable on a small scale and it only applies towards a specific area where this geofilter will be utilized. Therefore, a comic convention or a book convention could easily use this filter to grab some attention so that people could come and use a filter that they really like. Needless to say, you don't really want to use the stock images that they provide you as filters because then you won't have any true unique value to it. So, if you just hire somebody on Fiverr to create an image for you to utilize as a filter, you can generally get a very unique filter that'll target a specific area and create a very lucrative business hole for your customers to fall into.

CONVERTING FOLLOWERS

Share for Shares

This is going to be a really short section because there's really only three ways to convert followers from and to the Snapchat platform. The first way to convert followers is to actually get shares for shares. This refers to the fact that you can go to another small profile that is selling a product that's similar to yours and you can offer to share their products with your user base if they share your products with their user base. This allows a collective and united front to selling the products that you want on Snapchat and also building up a list on Snapchat so that you can sell even more products to. This is how you convert Snapchat users to Snapchat users that follow you.

Using Snap Chat as A Mailing List

You don't actually have to ever leave Snapchat unlike many of the products services like Facebook where you want to sell a product, but Facebook doesn't allow you to have a page where people can go and receive notifications so long as they are just signed up. Facebook requires that they select one of three view options: first on page, occasional, and never. Since Snapchat is more like a Facebook feed of friends, advertising on Snapchat is more like just posting a post on Facebook like you would with friends and families of your own. You can actually build a mailing list that solely relies on Snapchat itself, so you can send out products and have them sign up to your Snapchat account instead of an email list. Additionally, you can have the snap code that's on the back of the card and have them sign up via either email or Snap Chat. You can use Snapchat as a mailing list. A lot of people want to convert the people on Snapchat into a mailing list so that they can send out emails to them, but this is honestly not needed if you use Snapchat in the correct way. Additionally, there is a downside to using Snap Chat as an emailing service because Snapchat is a video platform that requires you to create a new ad every time you want to send out something to the public.

Essentially, the problem is that you can't create templates and you cannot send out automatic updates on Snapchat to run an email campaign that is automated. This is the true difference between Snapchat and the mailing list that you may have generated over the years. If you prefer the method of running an email campaign and getting people to sign up via email, then you may not want to switch over to Snapchat as your mailing list, but Snapchat generally provides you with a massive audience that is regularly invested in everything that they follow. Since each of the videos that they watch is usually consistent of the 10-second marker, they can watch almost all of them within the 30 minutes that the average user stays inside of the Snapchat application. Needless to say, it is up to you as to whether you want to switch individuals from your mailing list to your Snapchat or not. This brings us to the next option.

Mailing List to Snap Chat

Converting your mailing list to your Snapchat user following base is going to be a little difficult because a lot of people in your mailing list will likely either use Snapchat or not use Snapchat and if they don't like the Snapchat application then you're going to have an email list that you need to keep up along with your Snapchat profile.

This is something that you need to keep in mind whenever you're switching between either an email list or a Snapchat list or even both of them. The way you can get individuals from your email list to your Snapchat is to Simply say that you have a Snapchat and you would like them to follow but a better way is to actually incentivize them by providing a product that they might like that is in the form of a digital format so that it doesn't cost you anything. All you have to do is say that if you sign up to Snapchat and send you a message, you will reply with the digital content. It's very easy to implement and a lot of people will bite this bait.

CONCLUSION

In this section we're going to go over some very hard and cold facts that you may not like to hear but that you need to understand this before you begin investing in this platform. These topics are really sensitive due to certain aspects of how people market, how a marketing campaign can go wrong, and who you're marketing to. Additionally, this section also provides you with a deeper look into whether you should or should not invest into Snapchat during a given period of time.

The Internet is The Internet

The first topic that I have to cover is that the internet is the internet and once you put something on the Internet, you are likely never ever going to not see it somewhere else on the internet. Snapchat is famous for its 10 second rule and you can actually make the video go up to infinity nowadays, but most people stay with the 10 second rule simply because they like the thrill of having to catch that snap in the moment rather than later down the road. It's kind of like a Facebook video that you only have a certain time limit to see. A lot of people get in trouble because they believe in that 10 second rule and that the 10-second rule will only apply to those 10 seconds, but you have to realize that you are sending out a 10-second clip that is going to be viewed by people who have phone recorders. An easy way that someone records something is they simply look at somebody else's phone and sees how outrageous the snap is on the Snapchat account. Once they see how outrageous it is, they then take out their phone and go track down the outrageous snap so that they can video capture it and then upload it to the Internet so that it is permanent. There are thousands of cases of this, though only a few of them are blown up in the media. These cases are when an individual said something or did something on Snapchat and someone else managed to record the 10 second video that was not supposed to last for more than 10 seconds. In these cases, you have people who lost their jobs, who lost their businesses, and especially lost their followers. You must understand that when you put something on the Internet, you have to assume that what you are putting on the Internet is going to be on there permanently. If you do not control your

Snapchat profile and you happen to be slightly inebriated one night whenever you attempt to reach out to your audience and you say something inappropriate; that will most likely come back to bite you. You have to treat this like it is work because it honestly is. Snapchat is a platform where you can advertise your services or products to other people. So, you must treat it like it's a business and not a social media account. People post things on their social media account that can be slightly lewd or outrageous and then those same people end up suffering the consequences of their actions. This is why I wanted to talk about this topic because Snapchat is filled with younger individuals who are more than capable of recording those outrageous moments and sending it everywhere. Additionally, the reason why I wanted to cover it first was due to the fact that Snapchat is an emotionally invested platform by default and so whenever you create content for this platform, the content tends to be personal even though you're selling a product because it has to be organic or the individuals on the platform won't believe it. When you make something personal, you eventually get to the point where you are no longer taking it as a serious application of business and you begin to mix personal and business together into one application, which has had devastating effects for small businesses.

Snap Chat Take Photos Without You Knowing

Snapchat is a company itself and, it has to make money somehow, but many people didn't understand how Snapchat made money beyond the advertising that was inside of Snapchat. However, not everyone wants to advertise on Snapchat and it is quite obvious that they make it easy for advertisers to place their advertisement but also make it easy for the user to ignore those advertisements. Just like Google is always trying to find a new way to sell their product, you and me, Snapchat is also trying to find a way to sell its average user. The first thing that they did and something that many people got very angry over was that Snapchat takes a photo when you first click the power button to turn on your standby screen. The person's phone would take a picture without the person actually knowing it and it would be a picture of whatever was in front of them or whatever was behind them. Essentially, Snapchat got the ability to temporarily capture what that person was doing when they were looking at the phone and since most

people open their phones in personal areas and have unique facial

expressions that they don't normally have in front of the camera, these

photos were being used to determine the average age for Snapchat users

and many other rather invasive items when it comes to actually utilizing

applications. This shows that Snapchat doesn't care about the privacy

for an individual. You could have a cell phone environment with a

room that's dedicated to advertising. In other words, it's a room where

there's only a camera that's suitable for advertising purposes. There

should be no sensitive information on it, there should be no account

login information on it, and it should just be a phone that is dedicated to

the use of advertising on social media platforms like Snapchat and

Instagram because the two of them are rather similar in their purpose.

Snap Chat Does Not Actually Delete Content

Now, speaking of privacy concerns, Snapchat is also like

Google in that it doesn't delete its' data once it's got it. The company

has publicly stated before that if you take a photo on Snapchat and

decide to delete it or rely on Snapchat to auto-delete it after the 10 seconds, those photos and videos that you take are not going to be removed. Now, for the average individual that's no problem at all because what is Snapchat going to do with those types of photos other than just show advertisers what type of users might go to their platform? The problem is when you dig a little bit deeper, it becomes quite evident that they are not selling these items towards content developers, towards advertisers, but towards business owners themselves. What would you do if you had access to something considered to be private account where the individual was able to do countless number of things in front of the camera that could show their personality and where they might fit inside of a business? This is something that a lot of business owners at the higher levels like to invest into because it gives them the real person behind all the credentials and it tells them whether the person is going to be damaging or not. After all, 90% of our business is the company image and if the company image is not perfect for the customer, it hurts the bottom line sales and so businesses invest in these types of content grabs to let them know what type of an individual a person is. Additionally, Snapchat uses this data in features that it's going to come out with. A good example that recently came out just before releasing this book was an advertisement that stated that the image detection program had been tried against a billion faces and since there are only nine billion people on the planet. The government obviously wanted to know how they managed to get these photos. This is not the first example of a company that will give you a service and then also take the content that you put on that service and use it for its own purposes. It would be a bad business practice to let somebody use a free tool and for you to not also find a way to take that free tool and benefit from it. Why would you create a Google Docs that can compete with Microsoft Word if you could not sell the software suite to businesses and then also utilize the Google voice application in combination with that to grab more data to feed to your artificial intelligence that needs to process linguistics. There are several reasons why this business would be collecting the content on the device and why Snapchat doesn't actually delete any of the content, but it's also really important to understand that this kind of happens to be the first topic that we were talking about. What goes on the internet will likely stay on the internet and if you put some inflammatory stuff on your Snapchat account, you are not only going to hurt your business if teenagers catch you or other Snapchat users catch you; but also if Snapchat decides that it wants to sell that inflammatory content to a news organization or even your competitors.

Snap Chat is almost Exclusively for consumers under the age of 30

Another thing that you have to keep in mind whenever you're advertising on Snapchat is that you're not trying to relate to old people here. There is a very small section of the audience that is actually comprised of anyone under the age of 30. The average Snapchat individual is a college student that ranges in between their late teenage years to late twenties. Adult themed subjects, when it comes to the online advertising space, may get wonderful hits when you advertise a certain book on helping a college topic, but you might also get a horrible mess if you try to do the same with an advertisement about any type of above 30 prescriptions like Viagra. However, it's also important to realize that there's a better click ratio with these individuals if you get the right advertisements in front of them. According to some websites, the click rates for the average individual user that knows the brand that they're clicking on will be about 47% of the time that they see the ads. This means that if they know your brand, they are likely to actually click on it 50% of the time or one out of every two ads. Now if they don't know your brand then it's obvious that they're going to click less but, at the same time, the estimated amount is around 30%, which is not bad considering that's one out of every three advertisements and then you run that against the odds of getting a couple hundred to even thousands of individuals coming towards your product.

Know When Not to Invest

The last word of warning that I want to cover is that you need to understand when you're not going to be able to invest in this platform anymore. For many of us, we still utilized Facebook if only to contact the loved ones that live way too far away for our own good. Snapchat is a lot like Twitter in the fact that it will have a phase where there is an enormous number of individuals standing on the platform and then a couple years down the road the platform will seemingly bottom out in terms of advertisements. It's very important to pay attention to how many users are currently actually active on the Snapchat platform because teenagers have a nasty habit of hopping applications whenever they find something that they love and this is true of Myspace, Facebook, Twitter, Instagram, and now Snapchat. All of these are social media websites that were built around the individual at the time where the individual would find it really nifty to play around with the application to communicate with others. However, every single one of these has had a period where they start off small, end up growing exponentially quickly, and finally plateauing before they start to level out. Snapchat is just one application in this long trend of finding new ways to communicate with others. So, it's really important to know when Snapchat is going to be useful and when Snapchat is not going to be useful, which is why I created this small section. You want to look for when the users begin to drop by the hundreds and when you hear the news talk about a new social media application. You might have thought the first one was obvious but the second one is a little bit less obvious in that a lot of people don't see the two at the same time. Therefore, if you notice that Snapchat is excessively losing users and you want to know if it's time to leave the platform, simply look and see if any of the news outlets or blogs are talking about a new, hot social media application that everyone is using. This is when it's time to begin studying that new social media application but to not completely stop the investment in the previous application, but begin moving your users over to that platform over there and bring those individuals with you whenever you land on the platform. This is how you properly invest in an advertising platform and then move on to the next advertising platform.

I know that this is the end of the book and I know that we have gone over a ton of information in this book, but I want you to understand that Snapchat is just a media application. Advertising on Snapchat is just advertising on Facebook with a few twists, advertising on Instagram with a few twists, and advertising on YouTube with a few twists. The platforms are always seeking ways to provide real advertisements from brands who want to care about the users that they're advertising to. The core elements in these companies are trying to find ways for advertising companies to interact with users in a better format than the old 1990s version of turning on the TV. This is where you see six commercials before the start of the show and you just go wash some dishes until the commercials are done. They are finding ways to engage with other consumers so that it's easier not only to convince the customer to buy your product but it's also more personal from the company that selling it. Having said that, thank you for reading this book and I'll see you next time.

www.ingramcontent.com/pod-product-compliance
Lightning Source LLC
Chambersburg PA
CBHW071517210326
41597CB00018B/2801